Raphael De Cordova Lewin

What is Judaism?

Or, a Few Words to the Jews

Raphael De Cordova Lewin

What is Judaism?
Or, a Few Words to the Jews

ISBN/EAN: 9783337008000

Printed in Europe, USA, Canada, Australia, Japan

Cover: Foto ©Lupo / pixelio.de

More available books at **www.hansebooks.com**

A FEW WORDS TO THE JEWS.

BY

REV. RAPHAEL D'C. LEWIN.

NEW YORK:

D. APPLETON & CO.,

90, 92, and 94 GRAND STREET.

1870.

Stereotyped by LITTLE, RENNIE & CO.,
645 & 647 Broadway, New York.

TO

HIS JEWISH BRETHREN,

THROUGHOUT THE WORLD,

This Essay

IS,

WITH FEELINGS OF SINCERE REGARD,

RESPECTFULLY

DEDICATED

BY

THE AUTHOR.

.

PREFACE.

THE VOICE OF REASON IS THE VOICE OF GOD. With this earnest conviction deeply impressed upon my heart, the following pages have been prepared, and are now respectfully presented to the public.

I am aware, however, that in thus unreservedly declaring my full opinions on the absorbing subject of the Jewish religion, I am rendering myself liable to much severe and harsh criticism. My views will not only be opposed with much bitterness by hundreds of my co-religionists, but my motives will even be, either wilfully or innocently, misunderstood. My opponents will not be likely to deal very mercifully towards me in their judgment, while among my friends and well-wishers there will be found some (and I could easily name them, even now, as I write) who will be apt to regard this publication, if not, indeed, the writer, with feelings akin to distrust and dislike. Still, I hope and believe that among those who will read this little essay, there will be many who will endorse my sentiments, and give me credit for at least being sincere in my intentions. To them, therefore, a few words of explanation should be given as to the reasons which have influenced me to undertake so arduous a task, and the object which I hope to attain thereby.

The age in which we live is an age of reason, of inquiry, and of investigation. The Educated, as a rule, are no longer content to be led by the dictates of blind faith in any branch of human knowledge, and least of all, in religious belief. Political equality, civil and religious liberty, the march of civilization, the rapid strides which science is everywhere making, have all combined to remove the scales from the eyes of men and to lessen the immense power which, until lately, crafty priests and ecclesiastics have exercised over the minds of the populace. Among all religious denominations there is now a healthy agitation, and the tendency is to purify the Church of those spurious elements which were engendered in times of bigotry and superstition, and thus by degrees to lessen the bar which separates the children of one Eternal Father from each other. That there is still a large amount of intolerance and bigotry manifested in certain quarters which will sometimes lead to very lamentable results, is, unfortunately, but too true ; and while we deplore this fact, we not only can pray to Almighty God to remove this evil, this plague-spot from society, by bringing knowledge into those quarters, but we can ourselves diminish the evil by diffusing education among all classes, and by using every legiti-

mate and honest means at our command to sup-
press intolerance and bigotry in whatever shape they
may present themselves. But, thanks to God, the
miscalled orthodoxy of all creeds, which engenders sel-
fishness, exclusiveness, illiberality, and finally despotism
of the worst kind—that of the mind—is fast dying out,
sinking into the grave to which long ere this it should
have been consigned. Thus it happens that in this free
and glorious country, perhaps more than in any other,
the pure and holy principles of religion are becoming
widely understood, and the differences which still exist
among men upon religious points form no barrier to
the general peace and happiness. Every day the
field of religious thought is being explored, and as the
light of reason is the more reflected upon the scene,
so are the several unholy doctrines and dogmas ar-
rayed before the tribunal of intelligence, condemned
as follies and sentenced to oblivion. In this way do
the several religions of the world form subjects for
just criticism, and thus has Judaism among the others
been brought prominently to public notice. Yes,
Judaism, the religion which has been so long despised,
scorned, and trampled under foot, is now a matter of
grave importance in the eyes of the world, and in this
country especially is attracting the attention of thousands of our non-Jewish brethren. Doubtless this
agitation and curiosity have been produced partly
from the schism which exists in our midst, the sig-

nal triumphs which have attended the efforts of the
Reform School of Judaism, the magnificent tem-
ples which are being erected in almost every large
city, the noble charitable institutions which are so
largely supported by Reform Jews, and the action of
the Rabbinical conferences recently held in Europe
and in Philadelphia.   Be the cause however what it
may, it is a fact that we are now being closely observed
by our neighbors, who are evincing considerable desire
to become better informed about Jews and their religion.
" What is Judaism ? " is by no means an uncommon
question ; and that it should be a question is a matter
of no surprise.   Why should there not be a question
upon the subject, when so much has been done and
said to mystify the public, and when the Jews themselves indirectly assist in this mystification.

The very existence of the numerous factions and
sects in our midst, the different shades of opinion,
even in the same sect, the weekly ravings of the so-
called orthodox press, the incomprehensible inconsis-
tency of those who pretend to adhere to the traditions
of our race, must surely excite the wonder, and,
perhaps, even the amusement of the Christian world.
And when it is remembered that, although much has
been written about Judaism, and many learned works
have been published for the information of the world,
yet there is nothing in the vernacular of such a charac-
ter as to present within a moderate compass the full

principles, doctrines, views, object, and destiny of the Jewish religion, it is certainly not a matter of astonishment that so little should be known about our faith. To the majority of Jews themselves, this subject is, from the same cause, very imperfectly understood; and hence the great opposition which is made to the Reform School by many pious and well-meaning persons, who not only know nothing of the aim of Reform, but even have erroneous impressions as to what constitutes true orthodoxy, according to the Rabbins and the traditions of Israel. To supply this want, therefore—to place before the public a brief but thorough explanation of the principles of Judaism, in a style simple enough to come within the range of all—has this essay been prepared. In it will be found all that I believe to be included under the title of Judaism. I have endeavored faithfully to state my full views on the religion of my race; to point out carefully whatsoever I deem of importance, and to declare unreservedly what I consider to be incongruities, inconsistencies, and altogether abuses quite foreign to true Judaism.

Wherever, in the course of this essay, allusion has been made to the hypocritical deceptions of miscalled Orthodoxy, I wish it to be perfectly understood, that it is only the practices of mock orthodoxy which have been condemned, and not of real Orthodoxy. Against the truly pious and consistent orthodox Jew who religiously believes in the traditions of his people, in the infallibility of the Talmud, and who faithfully puts into practice all that he professes in theory, not one disrespectful word should be uttered. How much soever this steadfast adherence to the practices of the past—which in the reasonable mind have long ceased to be obligatory—may be deplored, the sincerity of the intention is eminently deserving of respect. It would be against the teachings of the Reform School, therefore, to condemn those who thus act up to what they believe. But to those violent fanatics from the ranks of a self-constituted orthodoxy, who profess one thing and perform another; who desert the ancient landmarks whenever fashion or convenience or worldly motives must be gratified, but who, nevertheless, clamor against every movement intended to advance the interests of Judaism; who denounce in public what they practise in private; who openly desecrate the most sacred commands, and yet revile Reformers as heretics; who substitute brute force for argument, passion for reason, and the fulmination of anathema for logical discussion; who by their outward sanctimonious mien and inward rebellious spirit, bring disgrace on the name of Jew—to them no explanation or apology is made. The masks which they have so long worn must now be torn down, and the utter nothingness of their professions exhibited to the public gaze and contempt.

To the truly orthodox as well as to the moderate reformer, I have only to say : Do not decide too hastily in your judgment of this essay. Read patiently the arguments, study carefully the references from the Scriptures and from history, weigh well the proofs, and let your Reason be your guide.

Whether the object of these pages will in any degree be accomplished, time alone will show. But whatever may be the result, I cannot be otherwise than conscious of having entered upon the task with pure feelings and with the earnest desire of benefiting my people and my religion. And so I hopefully send forth my little work among my brethren, and humbly implore the blessing of God on the issue.

R. D'C. L.

The Eclectic Collegiate Institute,
617 Lexington Avenue, cor. 53d St.,
New York, Dec., 1869.

WHAT IS JUDAISM?

.

HE night of religious persecution has forever passed; the morning light has dawned, and the Sun of Progress is shedding his refulgent rays upon the world, dispelling the clouds of darkness and illumining mankind with celestial truth, to the everlasting glory of Almighty God, and the eternal happiness of the human race. Yes, religious persecution is dead. It now lies numbered among the things which have been; it rests in the tomb of the past, and will never again be resuscitated. We pause not here to inquire as to the agencies which have been employed by an all-wise and directing Providence, in effecting this happy consummation. We seek not to ascertain the causes which have been instrumental in thus revolutionizing those very thoughts and opinions of men which for centuries had obtained such irresistible control over their actions. Enough for our purpose that truth has triumphed, that the inalienable rights of conscience have been acknowledged, that the being possessed of a heaven-born immortal soul, endowed with the high faculty of reason, blessed by God with the capacity to act according to the impulses of his own heart, is at length permitted by his fellow-being to exercise those divine rights which constitute him the child of God, is at length free to worship his Almighty Father and Creator, agreeably with the promptings of his own nature.

Glorious, indeed, have been the results produced by this revolution in religious thought. The minds of men, no longer enslaved by the tyranny of Church or State, assume now their legitimate powers, and regard all subjects as food for investigation and discussion. The claims of humanity are felt and acknowledged, irrespective of religious differences. The peculiar tenets held sacred by any man, occasion none to withhold from him the free enjoyment of those privileges to which, as a man, he is justly entitled. The state or commonwealth, which is made up of individuals and not of individual opinions, imposes no restraint on the liberty of the individual on account of his religious convictions ; and indeed in almost every country where the refining influence of modern civilization has penetrated, the same political rights and distinctions are shared in common by every man, notwithstanding his private views on religion, or the peculiar manner in which he may worship the God of his belief.

And now that this glorious epoch in the world's history has been fairly inaugurated, surely we Israel-

ites, above all others, should experience the purest
emotions of holy joy and the deepest feelings of gratitude, when we reflect on what has been and what
is now.   Religious freedom is indeed a sweet thing
to us.   Who can better appreciate it?   We have been
the martyrs of martyrs.   For eighteen unbroken centuries the world has conspired to hunt us down, to
torture and oppress us, to drive us without the pale
of humanity, to exterminate us from among men, or
compel us to disavow our blessed inheritance, and
swear allegiance to strange gods.   Truly no nation
upon the face of the earth has ever endured such sys-
tematic persecution, such relentless cruelties, such
fearful sufferings, as that nation to which, praised be
God, we have the honor of belonging.   What then
should be our bounden duty, now that God has given
us rest from our enemies, now that He has turned our
adversaries into our friends and brethren, now that
the world has so far advanced in religious knowledge
as to comprehend the great truth that conscience can
never be forced?   Surely it is, to adhere as steadfastly
to that hallowed faith in our prosperity as we did in
our adversity.   Surely it is, to remove all the impurities from that faith which, during those centuries of
persecution, bigotry, ignorance, and fanaticism, have
grown so thickly around it, as almost to hide its tran-
scendent beauties.   Surely it is, to understand that
faith according to its God-like purity, to transmit that

faith to our children as a priceless treasure, to proclaim that faith to the world, through the teachings of
our lives, and thus show that Judaism is indeed a
Religion emanating from the Deity himself, and that
none know better than Jews how to serve that Deity, or
how to fulfil those divine laws of universal love and
truth which He has framed for the government and
welfare of all his children upon earth.

But these duties are incumbent upon us, not alone
in order to evince our gratitude to God and our appreciation of the blessings of religious liberty, but
because, free as we may be, our faith has still its enemies, who, though powerless to harm, are yet powerful enough to detract from its excellences by painting
it in false colors and exhibiting it under a garb which
never belonged to it, in the hope thus to accomplish
by fraud and treachery what never could be accomplished by tyranny or oppression. Would you know
where to seek those enemies? Look for them *without*
our fold. Look for them *within* our fold.

Look for them *without* our fold, in the many conversion societies which disgrace the age in which we
live ; in the "so-called" societies for the diffusion of
the Gospel among the Jews, which infest our land,
and which are so zealously maintained by thousands
of foolish, bigoted men and women, who expend, an-
nually, fortunes upon the feeble attempt to convert
the Jews, and rejoice when some poor miscreant, who

has but little sense, still less honor and a great amount of poverty, falls into their clutches—fortunes which could be better bestowed upon the aged, the destitute, the widow, and the orphan of their own sects—fortunes which could aid in diffusing education among the ignorant masses of the Christian Church, and teaching the sublime lesson, that God is the Father of mankind, and that all men are alike his children and will be saved in Him.

Look for them *without* our fold, in the doctrines put forth every Sunday from too many of the Church pulpits ; doctrines which take hold upon the ignorant minds of the populace, and cause them to believe that Judaism is corruptive ; that Jews think it their duty to cheat and swindle their Christian neighbors ; that Jews must still be held responsible for the crucifixion of him whom the Gentile world revere as a Saviour, that all who believe not in him will be condemned to eternal perdition, and that therefore it is a meritorious action to convert the Jew, even if that conversion be accomplished by means not in themselves fair or honorable.

Look for them *within* our fold, in the unholy and ridiculous opinions entertained about Judaism by too many of its own followers ; in the follies and superstitions which have crept into Judaism, and which still cling to a portion of the House of Israel ; in the ignorant declarations of faith which are occasionally

2*

ushered into the world as being Judaism ; in the very
slight knowledge possessed by a large majority of our
people as to what really constitute the principles of
Judaism, and the duties of Jews.

Look for them *within* our fold, among the self-constituted leaders of the people, who, to accomplish their
own wicked ends, to gratify their own private animosi-
ties, to pander to their own intolerable vanities, or to
ensure their own private interests, labor earnestly to
depress, to mystify, to blind, to subjugate those who
look up to them for light and instruction.   Thus they
offer ignorance to the people, and call it knowledge ;
darkness, and call it light ; folly, and call it wisdom ;
deception, and call it honor.

Shall we then be silent, when our sacred heritage is
being thus trifled with ?   Shall we hold our peace
when our pure and spotless religion is being thus
assailed by enemies *without* our fold and by enemies
within our fold ?   Shall they who hold the exalted and
responsible positions of teachers of God's Holy Word,
allow themselves to be intimidated or awed, because
their enemies happen to be strong or many ?   Shall
the guides of the people whom God has appointed to
work out the happiness of His children, prostitute their
holy office because worldly wisdom would tell them,
"Do not jeopardize your own temporal interests ?"
They who dare listen to such admonitions, they who
dare betray their sacred trust, they who dare think

more of themselves than of the duty they owe their
Master, are unworthy of their calling, unworthy their
lineage, unworthy their mission, and merit the scorn
and indignation of every right-minded man.

We are those teachers ; we are those guides ; we,
Israelites whom God has appointed as "a covenant of
the people, a light of the nations."[1]

Let us then go forth against our enemies "in the
name of the Lord of Hosts." Let us raise above us ·
the banner of our mission—Truth—holy, divine,
heavenly Truth ! Let us battle with our enemies
without our fold and *within* our fold, for we can fight
them both, even at the same time, and all the arms
that will be necessary, are but a perfect knowledge of
our faith, and a firm determination to live in accordance with that knowledge ; and while thus giving practical illustrations of the recondite beauties of Judaism,
we will most signally defeat our enemies, and victo-
riously return from the strife, having benefited ourselves, improved mankind, advanced the interests of
pure religion, and promoted the honor and glory of
the Eternal God of Heaven and Earth.

Come, then, Israelites, let us examine our faith by
the light of reason and intelligence. Let us not be
afraid to handle it—it will bear investigation. Let us
not hesitate to test our religion. If it will not meet the
test, it is unworthy the name of Religion. If we shrink
from testing it, we are unworthy the name of Jews.

Come, then, with hearts and minds bent upon this holy task. Come with the firm resolution to abide by the consequences. Come in the name of God, in the name of Religion, in the name of Truth, and let us ask ourselves the all-important question, What is Judaism ?

In order to solve this question satisfactorily, we must, in the first place, be certain as to the sources whence we have derived our religion. These sources are three in number : 1st, Reason ; 2d, Nature ; and 3d, Revelation.

Without reason, truth could not exist upon earth, for it is only through the agency of our reason that we are enabled even to comprehend the very fact of our existence. A renowned Jewish philosopher has said, "The angel that communicates between God and man is man's reason."[2] So also a profound thinker of modern times has asserted, "On earth there is nothing great but man ; in man there is nothing great but mind."[3]

These are powerful assertions, and they are true. Man is the masterpiece of creation, and it is only his reason which makes him so. Man only, of all God's works, is capable of understanding that he has been created, and it is only his reason which gives him that capacity. "Man," says the great Pascal, "is but a reed,—the very frailest in nature ; but he is a reed that thinks. It needs not that the whole universe

should arm to crush him.   He dies from an exhala-
tion, from a drop of water.   But should the universe
conspire to crush him, man would still be nobler than
that by which he falls ; for he knows that he dies ;
and of the victory which the universe has over him,
the universe knows nothing.   Thus our whole dignity
consists in thought." [4]

Reason, therefore, above everything else, must be
the source whence man derives knowledge.   Possessed, then, of this reason, his attention is directed
to the wonders of creation.   He beholds and reflects.
Nature speaks aloud to him through her innumerable
voices, and becomes the second great source whence
he derives religious knowledge.   And nature is indeed
a noble instructor.   Who, possessed of reason, can
fail to see, in the mighty works of nature by which we
are constantly surrounded, the goodness and greatness
of an all-wise Creator ?   Who can be so dull as not
to receive invaluable lessons from the many grand
objects which are found in the external world ?   Who
can pass through this life, beholding, reflecting, and
understanding, and not see, in nature, nature's God ? [5]

From Reason and Nature, then, Revelation is developed, and man's religious belief is formed.   But
this revelation is by no means a sudden result of the
other sources.   It is a progressive work.   As God is
the Creator of the human race, so also is He the
Educator of that race ; and as man's greatest happi-

ness consists in continual development and progression,[6] it has pleased Him to make known his will gradually, and to choose certain agents through whom the happiness of man may be secured, and His gracious will made the permanent inheritance of all His children. Thus was this education of the human race commenced by God's communicating His will, through the means of Revelation, first to Adam, then to Abraham and the Patriarchs, and subsequently to their descendants, the children of Israel, whom God has chosen to be his missionaries upon earth, and the guides of all his children to the shrine of Religion.[7]

Herein consists the grand mission of Israel. Not for our weal alone did it please God to bestow this commission upon our race, not that our prosperity or happiness alone may result therefrom, not that these blessed truths should be monopolized by any one race or set of God's children, as the inalienable right of that one race or set of men, and the right of none else besides. No ! exclusiveness forms no feature in Israel's mission.[8] Israel is the chosen of the Lord only for the purpose of bringing spiritual happiness to the world. Otherwise God has no chosen people. All are his people, all are his creatures, all are his children, hence all are chosen by him. As the universal Father, God loves the beings formed by his creative hand, and seeks to promote the happiness of all alike. The means, however, for the accomplishment of this,

are known alone to Him, and so He has willed that
Israel should become His missionaries upon earth, in
order to cause the light of divine truth to shine upon
the world, and thus conduce to the happiness of all,
by imparting truth as the common inheritance of
mankind.

* From the three sources—Reason, Nature. and Revelation—our knowledge of Judaism is obtained ; and
from these three sources also we learn that Judaism
exists under two phases, according to both of which
separate definitions are necessary.   The first is its
Eternal phase. and may be thus defined :

Judaism is the grand universal system of all the
religious truths necessary for man to believe, and of
all the moral laws which God in His inscrutable wisdom and goodness has framed for the government of
his children upon earth. in order that through the
belief in these truths, and the observance of these
laws, every human being may become good. and consequently happy, and thus approach that state of perfection which is the highest pinnacle of godliness and
of supreme felicity.

In this sense, Judaism is Religion in the purest
conception of the word, for the belief in these truths.
and in the necessity for practising these laws, which
together constitute the very essence of Judaism, in-
spires the soul of man with an indescribable longing
to soar upward to the Great Spirit of spirits, the

Almighty Fountain of truth and purity and wisdom ;
and while thus inspiring it, renders it conscious how
impossible it is ever to completely attain that exalted
summit to which it will, nevertheless, continually
aspire.   And this is indeed Religion.

True, genuine religion, is nothing else but the term
whereby we understand that exaltation of the soul,
which recognizes its own superiority, while at the
same time it is forced to confess its own finiteness and
dependence.

True, genuine religion, is nothing else save that
intense and earnest longing of the divine spirit placed
by God into man, after the Noblest, the Purest, the
Highest—that unconquerable desire to look up to the
Infinite Being, as the embodiment of perfection—that
fervent attachment, love, and veneration for the Author of all—that devout and constant wish to come
into perfect connection with Him—that deep humility
with which it acknowledges the impossibility of such
intimate connection, and feels the immense distance
which must still exist, how near soever it may approach.

Thus Judaism and Religion are synonymous terms.

But Priests and dogmatists of all sects have endeavored to give other definitions of them.   For Religion
is represented as being the offspring of the Bible, the
work of Revelation alone, the communication of doctrines through supernatural agencies, the entire immo-

lation of our own reason, thoughts, and feelings upon
the altar of faith, the firm adherence to certain set
formulas of creed and such other manifestations of
piety whereby the love of God may be gained or his
anger avoided. And as for Judaism, very many of its
own followers and friends, to say nothing of its enemies, will not allow it to be a creative power at all ;
nay, will not even allow it to be a spiritual power, but
zealously labor to associate with it traditional edicts
and observances, forms and ceremonies, and a rigid
adherence to everything which time has honored by
the name of Judaism. Thus we find, even at the
present day, the grossest follies and superstitions being put forward by a certain school of bigots,—
who wear the sanctimonious mien of religion merely
to screen the defects of their own private lives,—as the
religion of our race, the religion which is destined by
God to become the religion of the world. Thus
Judaism is by these self-constituted, self-opiniated,
ignorant, pseudo-orthodox Jews, deprived of its holy
spirit, and sent forth into the world, shorn of everything which may proclaim it *the* Religion, and retain-
ing only those customs and laws which the exigences
of certain times rendered necessary for the preservation of the inward spirit, but which have long since
become obsolete—to the detriment of the interests of
Judaism, and the mental debasement of Jews. Whereas Judaism is indeed pure Religion, and Religion is

3

indeed far exalted above such conceptions. For it is Religion which has formed the Bible, and not the Bible which has formed Religion. Religion is life. Religion is the common inheritance of humanity. Religion lives with man, and is a portion of his nature. It has been, is now, and will forever remain an everlasting monument of the very existence and truth of God himself.

Having, then, arrived at the proper definition of Judaism, as regarded from its eternal phase, let us direct our attention to those religious truths imparted by Judaism, and which are the only truths which man need believe in. These truths are all the doctrines which Judaism teaches us about God, the World, and Man.

Concerning God, we are taught to believe that He is Spirit,[9] Most Holy and Pure,[10] Incorporeal and Indivisible,[11] Eternal and Immutable,[12] One and only One, to whom none can be compared, to whom no likeness can be ascribed;[13] Omnipotent,[14] Omniscient,[15] and Omnipresent,[16] All-Good, but All-Just,[17] Supremely Intelligent,[18] Merciful[19] and Beneficent,[20] the Great "I am,"[21] the Beginning and the End,[22] the First and the Last,[23] the Reason, the Life, and the Motion of all beings,[24] the Producer of everything,[25] the Eternal King, Lord, Ruler, and Preserver of the world,[26] the only Creator,[27] and the sole Saviour of mankind.[28]

This peculiar Jewish conception of God is the cardinal truth upon which all other truths are based. It is the grand centre to which everything else converges. It is the first great step toward religious perfection, the point from which all other doctrines must emanate.

Concerning the world, Judaism teaches us that it owes its origin to God ;[29] that he called all the materials which compose it into existence, created the forces, and ordained the laws through which everything in the world performs its appointed object ;[30] that these forces and laws are wisely arranged in order to give regularity and harmony to all things, and thus form the Universe into a perfect whole ;[31] that there exists no absolute evil in nature, since everything has its purpose, and that purpose is a wise and good one, calculated to produce the greatest advantages to mankind at large ;[32] that even where our ignorance of the workings of Nature may make us regard some things as evil, yet they only seem so to us, but are in reality features in that government which is intended for the general weal ;[33] that the world itself was called into existence so as to produce happiness, and so that there might be objects upon whom God could lavish His infinite love, and thus cause His creatures to rejoice in Him, and be supremely happy in His gracious favor.[34]

This idea of the world blended, with the sublime idea of God, naturally leads us to the contemplation

of Man, the noblest work of creation, for whose bene-
fit the world has been created.

Upon this subject—Man—we are taught to believe
that God has endowed him with a nature essentially
higher than any other being, for where all other creatures are but material beings, man possesses an immortal soul which continues to live after the dissolu-
tion of the body, and thus partakes in some degree
of the spirit of God.[35] And not only in his twofold
nature is man superior, but even in his material form ;
for he bears upon him the impress of divinity, and
is the only being gifted with the power of speech.
Through his spiritual nature, man inherits reason and
conscience, by means of which, combined with the
power of free will, he is enabled to develop his intellectual faculties and thus become perfect ; to conform
his conduct to the will of God, and thus become happy.[36] But as in consequence of the union between
body and soul, a continual struggle between the animal and spiritual propensities will forever continue in
the breast of man, it is impossible for him, during his
earthly life, to attain the summit of perfection.[37] He
will fall into sin, although he is not compelled to do
so, since sin can be subdued by the strong will of his
spirit.[38] When man sins, therefore, he loses for the
time his God-like nature, and receives his punishment
in this very loss.[39] But he is able to regain his former
eminence, through the medium of repentance.[40] Thus

man carries the mediator between himself and God in his own heart.

All that is necessary for his forgiveness and his restoration to his original position, is sorrow on his part for the sin which he has committed, and a sincere amendment of his conduct in the future.

Thus man's highest destiny is to triumph over his material propensities, and thereby elevate his God-like nature, which will in return elevate him ; and this he is enabled to do through his knowledge of those Divine Truths concerning God, the World, and Man, and by being thoroughly conversant with those Moral Laws which God has framed for the government of His children upon Earth.

The moral laws prescribed by Judaism teach us our duty to God, to our fellow-men, and to ourselves.

To God, in regarding Him as the Highest Good, in loving,[41] adoring,[42] and obeying[43] Him with all the energy of which we are capable. To love God, we must love all that He loves. The world and its contents have been made for man because God loves man, hence we also must love man, and strive to promote his happiness. To love God we must love virtue, and must always practise what our heart tells us will be pleasing to God ; and by so doing we again fulfil our destiny, for we will become happy in the very thought of God, and our spirit will then soar upward to Him and aspire to perfection.[44]

3*

To adore God, we must feel that notwithstanding our superiority we are yet but very insignificant beings when compared to Him, and that therefore it becomes us humbly to trust in Him, to believe in His goodness, wisdom, and justice in all things, and to pray to Him, so that through the power of prayer, our natures may be strengthened, our souls invigorated, and thus be the better enabled to triumph over sin, so as to accomplish our destiny and be happy here and hereafter.[45]

To obey God, therefore, becomes only the consequence of loving and adoring Him, and this we must do by observing all those duties contained in the Religious Truths and in the Moral Laws taught by Judaism.

Our next duties are those we owe our fellow-men, and these are embodied in the Divine precept : "Thou shalt love thy neighbor as thyself." To fulfil these duties we must abstain from doing or saying anything against our fellow-men, which we would not like them to do or say against us. We must be just in all our actions, and as fair in our dealings with others as we would like others to be with us. We must perform acts of charity and benevolence,[46] we must be kind and forgiving,[47] we must be forbearing and tolerant ;[48] and in the performance of all these duties we must never forget that, as all men are God's children, we are bound to regard all men as brothers, irrespective of creed or nationality.[49]

By a faithful observance of these duties, we will be enabled to fill worthily all the social stations of life, and in our relations to our fellow-beings bring happiness on them and happiness on ourselves, and thus place us on the road to perfection, which is the grand object of religion.

With these duties toward God and our fellow-men, we have also duties to perform to ourselves.

The chief of these is, to use all our energies and faculties for the attainment of our God-like destiny. We must therefore cultivate our minds, and store them with all the treasures of learning, as far as we have the ability.[50] But especially must we acquire religious knowledge, for that is the greatest of knowledge, since it leads us to perfection.[51] We must be industrious, temperate, and patient ; holy in our thoughts, holy in our feelings, and endeavor to attain happiness on earth and eternal happiness in the future world by observing all the laws of our Maker, and feeling that the nearer we in our lives approach unto Him, the nearer are we to that state of perfection and happiness for which we are intended.[52]

This, then, is our Religion.

And now we ask, where is there a belief so true, so pure, so godly as Judaism ? Is not Judaism Religion ? Is not Judaism life, spirit ? Has it not the stamp of God upon it ? Surely it is a great power, a power which has been working from time immemorial, a power which will forever work, animating mankind, reforming mankind, elevating mankind, and glorifying mankind with its hallowed influence.

Thus far have we considered the first phase of Judaism, which is the greater, for it is its eternal phase. It is under this phase that Judaism becomes pure religion, and that we as Jews become God's missionaries upon earth to teach mankind the knowledge of their Father, and his word of truth.

There is yet another phase, however, under which Judaism is of peculiar interest to us as Jews alone, and this is its temporal phase. But before we proceed to examine Judaism according to this phase, some preliminary remarks are necessary.

Religion lives with man and is a portion of his nature. At no time since the creation of the world has this power been inoperative. Long before the Bible was written, Religion exercised its influence and gave repeated manifestations of its existence. Thus in the life of the very first man, we find the religious sentiment recognizing God and feeling the immensity of His Spirit. In the picture presented to us of the early happiness of Adam, previous to his having yielded to his material propensities, we discover his religious nature rejoicing in the love of God and soaring up toward Him in humble recognition of its own superiority, and yet of its own dependence. And when, having sinned, we hear him confessing, "Thy voice

I heard in the garden and I was afraid,"[53] we again perceive the influence of religion in the power of his conscience, which makes him feel ashamed to meet his God and bitterly reproaches him for his sin. So also when Abel in grateful appreciation of the blessings of God offers up to Him a portion of his earthly treasures, he is actuated by the promptings of his religious nature, which at that early age associated the worship of God with the presentation of gifts, in the hope thereby to propitiate His favor.[54] Again, when jealousy and envy combine to produce the unnatural crime of fratricide, we hear the voice of Religion pronouncing the great truth : "Sin lieth at the door, and unto thee is its desire, but thou canst rule over it."[55] At a later period of the world's history the religious sentiment of man becomes more purified, and Abraham perceives in God, not the Being who is alone vested with Supreme power, not the Being who covets sacrifice and desires the debasement of his creatures, but the Infinite God of Love, who having created man in His own divine image, who having bestowed upon him an immortal soul, which is capable of being elevated to the highest point of honor, delights to see him elevating that soul and ennobling those feelings which constitute his God-like nature.[56] Following in the path of religious thought traced out for them by their illustrious progenitor, the Patriarchs continue the holy work of disseminating religious knowledge

and impressing mankind with the true belief in God.[57]
And at length arises the immortal legislator who is
destined by God to establish a nation and to give that
nation laws and statutes, which while preserving its
nationality and rendering it distinct and peculiar
among all nations, as long as it was necessary for its
nationality to be preserved, would, at the same time,
give it the capacity to receive and retain those divine
truths and those moral laws which form the very essence of religion, and thus cause it to become so
thoroughly permeated with the pure spirit of Religion,
as to enable it, not alone to exist without the aid of
those national laws and statutes, but also to conquer
the world and bring all mankind to the same state of
religious truth, and so place the entire human race on
the road to perfection and supreme happiness.

Thus it is Religion which has formed the Bible, and
not the Bible which has formed Religion.

But to what advantage were those national laws and
statutes, if in themselves they form not the principle
of religion?

The history of the human race incontestably proves
that religion has existed among all nations, how crude
or imperfect soever their moral and intellectual culture
may have been.[58] But because religion has always
lived with man and will forever live with man, and
because man is a creature of progression requiring
time to develop his higher faculties, and because this

development being essential to happiness will be eternal, Religion manifests itself in a people according to that people's moral and intellectual standard. The great power of the religious sentiment, innate in the breast of man, is to direct his attention to a Superior Being, and to make him feel that it is his duty to worship that Being. But upon this very worship Religion assumes different phases, according to the development of its votaries and the times in which they live. Thus, in connection with the spirit of religion, arose those outward manifestations of religious feeling, which tending to familiarize man with the spirit and to promote the great end of religion—human perfection and happiness—have also assumed the name of religion, and have come to be regarded as such through the force of association. At first, however, these outward manifestations had no intention of rendering the mind familiar with the spirit of religion, but were intended solely to give expression to the religious feeling which then regarded worship as its chief end and aim. Thus among all rude and uncivilized nations the idea of God is associated with the idea of a superior power, before which the inferior must bow and pay homage. Hence came sacrifices, which formed the most conspicuous feature in the worship of ancient nations. The end to be gained by these sacrifices was the propitiation of the Deity, the idea being that by offering up to Him something which was prized very dearly, by depriving themselves of what they valued most, by enduring privations and sufferings, they might either appease His wrath or win His favor. The rudest form of giving expression to this feeling was in human sacrifice. All those nations which were plunged into barbaric heathenism, regarded this form as the greatest token of piety and reverence for their gods.⁰⁰ But this is indeed the very lowest degree of religious feeling, for this misconception of the Divine Being tends to degrade man by forcing him to do violence to his natural feelings and affections.

Now it must be remembered that when Judaism made its appearance, the entire world was in darkness upon the subject of spiritual religion. The religious feeling could not grasp anything higher than the conception of a God and the recognition of his power. It had yet to be trained to see in God the perfection of purity, the embodiment of love. It was this task which Judaism had to perform in its earliest days. But as to accomplish this, was to introduce into the world a new idea, and as all new ideas, especially in the field of religious thought, have to battle with old established customs and predilections, it would have been impossible for Judaism to have entered upon its mission of reforming the world, without being invested with an outward covering of a coarser nature, so as to protect it in the struggle which it would have to

encounter.   Especially was this necessary when we
recollect that the Israelites, who were to be the depositaries of this Idea, were themselves undeveloped and
uncultivated.

True, in religious feeling they were very superior
to their neighbors, for they recognized in God a Unit,
and knew that human sacrifice was murder ; but still,
having for years witnessed the debasing rites of the
Egyptians, they were entirely unable to comprehend
the abstract idea of religion ; and the very Idea would
have been crushed out even among themselves, had it
not been for its coat of mail, in which it was purposely
enveloped."   Hence those national laws and statutes
which Moses imparted to the children of Israel, were
of considerable advantage, and even bore the sanction
of God, since they acted as the preservers of the Religious Idea, and were well calculated to serve as the
means to the end.   Thus have we Judaism in its
temporal phase, and according to the considerations
already given we are enabled to define it as follows :

Judaism is that peculiar system of Religion which
embraces all those national laws and statutes prescribed
by Moses, the founder and legislator of the Jewish
nation,—for the Jews alone, and obligatory only upon
them, so that by means of those national laws and
statutes, the minds of the people may become more
purified, and the people holier and more sanctified,
and thus be the better prepared to retain and pro-

mulgate those Divine Truths and Moral laws which constitute the very essence of pure Judaism and of pure Religion.

Very many of these statutes have lost their practicability since the overthrow of the Jewish nation as a body politic, and the destruction of the Temple. And this is, above all, the greatest proof of the truth of our religion. The Idea is capable of living without its material covering.

These national laws and statutes, be it remembered, were intended by the legislator only to serve as the means to the end ; they were never to usurp the place of the spirit of Religion ; they were not destined to be eternal, but yet they had the sanction of the Deity, and are obligatory upon Israelites as long as they effect the purpose for which they were intended.

As soon, however, as Reason has decided that the time for their observance has passed, that they no longer effect their purpose, that according to the age in which we live, the religious Idea, if requiring an outer covering at all, needs one of different materials ; then the observance of them has forever passed, and a continuance of them is but a violation of those grand eternal principles which constitute pure Judaism.

To such class belong the laws of sacrifices. Animal sacrifice, though not so degrading and immoral as human sacrifice, is yet but a token of a very low religious state of feeling. Sacrifice was never com-

manded by Judaism ; it was only tolerated. The
Israelites, rude and uncivilized as they were when they
left the chains of the Egyptian serfdom, could not
naturally have been expected to have shaken off, at the
very commencement of their religious career, a custom
which every nation regarded as pertaining to religion,
and one which they had witnessed for centuries. Hence
to have deprived them of this means of giving expression to their religious sentiment would again have
been to have crushed out the Idea immediately : so
sacrifices were tolerated, but only tolerated. As soon
as the proper moment arrived, the best of Israel's
leaders denounced them. Thus the Prophets—Israel's
greatest reformers—continually inveighed against the
sacrificial observances ; and indeed to such an extent
did Jeremiah carry his opposition to this mode of degrading the Divine Being and the divine nature of
man, that he actually contradicted the very assertions
of Moses, for where the legislator had sanctioned sacrifices in the name of the Lord, Jeremiah declared
with remarkable emphasis—"I spake not unto your
fathers, saith the Lord, nor commanded them, when
I brought them out of the land of Egypt, concerning
burnt-offerings or sacrifices."[61] We, at this age, can
perfectly understand that Jeremiah's words were not
contradictory to Moses' ; since Moses, also, knew the
baneful consequences of sacrifices, and only permitted
them through the force of circumstances, and because

Religion lives with man, and must adopt such outward manifestations as the state of man's intellect permits ; but surely at the age when Jeremiah lived, his words to the Israelitish nation must have seemed little better than rebellion against the very word of God.

Yet did the sacrifices fall. During the second Temple, in which sacrifices were continued, houses of Prayer arose as rivals to the Temple, and became infinitely above it in real religious importance.[52] And why was this? Because sacrifices had entirely lost their hold upon the Jewish people. The nation had developed and could well sustain the religious Idea without the aid of sacrifice. As soon therefore as the Second Temple is destroyed, sacrifice vanishes forever, and is lost to the Jewish people as it is to the world. If then we attempt to establish religion upon the basis of sacrificial worship, if we attempt to assert that sacrifice has only vanished for a time, and must be commemorated by certain additional prayers and ceremonies, if we attempt to look back upon the ancient mode of worship with feelings of regret, and long for a return of such worship—then indeed are we little better than the rabble who came forth from Egypt ; then indeed do we long for a relapse into heathenism, and become unworthy to continue our mission of promulgating God's Word of Truth.

SACRIFICE *is* DEAD. THE JEWISH NATIONALITY AS A SEPARATE POLITICAL ORGANIZATION *is* OVERTHROWN.

THE BELIEF IN THE RESTORATION OF ISRAEL TO THE
LAND OF THEIR FATHERS, AND THAT THE REDEEMER
WILL COME TO ZION, *is* AN EXPLODED THEORY ; AND GOD
BE PRAISED FOR ALL HIS MERCIES.

To such class also belong the Dietary Laws, which
indeed were very valuable for the people to whom
they were given, in the age in which they existed, and
for the countries for which they were intended. As
sanitary laws, they are even now of importance at certain seasons of the year and in certain climates, but
that they are Religious Laws, or that they were ever
intended as such, the very spirit of Religion de-
nies.

To such class also belong all those laws which have
reference to the political government of the Israelitish
nation, which being no longer in existence, the laws
themselves are of course inoperative.

And now we will consider those laws and statutes
which have not yet lost their practicability, but which
form Judaism according to its temporal phase, and
will continue to be obligatory upon Israelites, until
history has set them aside.

These laws may be divided into two classes : 1st,
The Holy Seasons, and 2d, The Ceremonies.

The Holy Seasons are those days and especial
portions of the year appointed for rest, prayer, and
reflection. They are : 1. The Sabbath ; 2. The Three
Festivals, Passover, Pentecost, and Tabernacles ; and

4*

3. The Two Great Holy Days, New Year and Day of Atonement.

The Sabbath is the fundamental statute of Judaism. Through its observance we are the better enabled to realize and appreciate all the blessings which are conferred by those divine truths and moral laws which constitute pure religion. The Sabbath is one of the greatest means of sanctification, because it relieves us from the yoke of worldly labor, invigorates our minds and bodies, thereby rendering them better fitted for the duties of life, and affords us the opportunity of reflecting upon the goodness of God, the beauty of His works, the wisdom of His laws, and our own God-like nature and heavenly destiny. Symbolically, the Sabbath is a type of what a good man's life should be every day ; but as labor is the lot of man, as he is wisely compelled to work for his living, and as many have indeed to toil with all their energies for the means of providing for the necessities of themselves and families, the Sabbath literally becomes a day of rest, a day of comfort, and above all, a day of holiness. It is the oldest religious institution, for it is coeval with the creation. It commemorates that august event, proclaims God as the sole author of the universe, and reminds us of the glorious mission which it has pleased God to bestow upon us.

To Israelites, therefore, the observance of the Sabbath is especially obligatory ; and to fulfil our duty in

this respect, we must abstain from the usual avocations of the week by which we earn our liveli-
hood, and devote the day to communion with our
Heavenly Father, to meditation on the excellencies of
religion, to rational and innocent pleasures, and to
those domestic and social enjoyments which are so
pleasing in the sight of the Beneficent Parent of
mankind."

The Festivals represent God as the Preserver and
Ruler of the World, and are intended to be vivid
testimonies of that love and benevolence so constantly manifested by Him towards all His creatures.
They are accordingly affixed to those seasons of the
year when the protecting power of God is especially
visible. At the same time they commemorate important events in the past history of Israel, and proclaim God as the Guardian of Israel, who watches
over His chosen people and protects them from the
machinations of their enemies, so as to accomplish
through their instrumentality His glorious design of
universal happiness and perfection.

The Festival of Passover, called also the Feast of
Unleavened Bread and the Feast of Redemption, is
celebrated in the season of Spring, at the time of the
ripening of the grains in the land of Palestine.

Its observance commences on the eve of the fifteenth
day of the first month, *Nisan*, and continues seven
days. Of these, however, only the first and last days

are considered holy. The Festival is the birthday feast of liberty, and is commemorative of Israel's deliverance from Egyptian bondage. As such, its annual return is hailed with feelings of joy and gratitude ; the more so, as with the event of this redemption our nation entered upon the discharge of its heavenly mission, and went forth into the world as the religious teachers of mankind.

Its name, Pasach or Passover, is derived from the sacrificial repast prepared by our forefathers on the eve of their redemption, in token of their faith in the promised deliverance. It is termed the feast of Unleavened Bread on account of the Mosaic command, by virtue of which nothing leavened was to be eaten during the Festival, in order to commemorate the exodus of the Israelites from Egypt, which was effected in such haste as to prevent them from even leavening the dough which they had taken with them at their departure. The most important portion of the Festival is the first night, because it commemorates that august occasion when "with a strong hand and an outstretched arm" the Lord God broke the iron bonds of tyranny, and proclaimed freedom as the inalienable right of man. For this reason it has ever been the pious custom in Israel to celebrate that night with songs of praise and thanksgiving, and to render the home a temple of devotion, wherein the memory of an event so fraught with the most glorious results to the world at large, may be cherished by those who are the depositaries of the true religious idea and of God's holy word of truth.[64]

The Festival of Pentecost is celebrated on the sixth day of the third month, Sivan, which is the fiftieth day after the first day of Passover. It is held in the season of harvest, and originally had no other significance than that of celebrating the conclusion of the harvest, which, in the land of Palestine, usually lasted fully seven weeks. For this reason it is called Shabuoth, or "Feast of Weeks." Religious solemnities and rejoicing were the characteristics of the Festival, and during the existence of the Jewish nationality and the Temple in Jerusalem, two full measures of fine flour had to be prepared into sacrificial bread as an offering of gratitude. Hence, the Festival is termed also the "Feast of the Full Harvest," and the "Feast of the First Offering." The Mishna furthermore called it "Azereth," or "Festival of Conclusion," having reference to the conclusion of the harvest.[65]

In later times, however, another and very important significance became attached to this Festival, for a historical reminiscence connected with Israel's mission was introduced, which gave it additional sanctity. This was no other than the memory of the Decalogue, which, through the power of inspiration, figuratively represented in the Bible by the revelation on Mount

Sinai, was communicated to Israel as the root and foundation of all religion, to be, by them, transmitted to all the inhabitants of the world.

The connection between the memory of this event and the harvest feast is perfectly natural, for aside from the consideration that the delivery of the Ten Proclamations is supposed to have taken place on the fiftieth day after the exodus of the Israelites from Egypt, these Divine Commandments constitute the richest spiritual harvest which man has ever received. Upon them every system of theology has been established. They have been, and will forever remain, throughout all times and generations, sufficient to nourish and sustain the religious idea in the mind of man. Of their inestimable value, all religious denominations which claim to partake of civilization are living witnesses. "They represent to us," writes a celebrated Christian divine, "both in fact and in idea, the granite foundation, the immovable mountain on which the world is built up, without which, all theories of religion are but as shifting and fleeting clouds; they give us the two homely fundamental laws, which all subsequent revelation has but confirmed and sanctified—the law of our duty towards God, and the law of our duty towards our neighbor." **

The Festival of Tabernacles is held in the seventh month, Tishri, and lasts seven days. It commences on the fifteenth, and ends on the twenty-first; but the

first day is the only one which is sacred. Celebrated as
an autumnal festival, at that peculiar season of the year
when the ingathering of all the productions of the
fields takes place, it truly becomes a festival of gratitude
and of thanksgiving to God for the innumerable
favors which He so lavishly bestows upon His children.
At the same time the Festival is intended to commemorate the especial goodness of God in preserving
our forefathers during the forty years they wandered in
the wilderness, prior to their entry in the land of Palestine. In order more forcibly to impress this event
upon our minds, the Bible ordains the dwelling in
booths or temporary houses, by virtue of which the
Festival derives its name as the Festival of Tabernacles
or Booths.

The day immediately following the seventh day is
termed Azereth, or the concluding feast, and is also
kept holy. The intervening days between the first
day of Tabernacles and the Azereth feast are half holy-
days similar to the intervening days between the first
and last days of Passover, and are called Chol Hamoed.
On these days the usual business avocations of life are
permitted. The entire Festival, together with the
ceremonies observed on the occasion, symbolically
represent the rich blessings which God in His goodness is pleased to bestow upon man through the
workings of Nature. They appeal to the imagination,
inspire the heart with sentiments of love and devotion,

and proclaim the Eternal Creator as the great, good,
pure, and holy Father of all, who, loving the beings
formed by His creative hand, and seeking to promote
their happiness, adopts the surest means for accom-
plishing this end, and makes all nature subservient to
His will."

The two great holy-days are not intended either to
refer to certain natural phenomena or to commemorate
historical events in the life of Israel, but they are
founded on the moral nature of man, and on those
peculiar qualities which render man human. The
union between body and soul, the intimate connection
between the physical and spiritual propensities often
engenders sin, and makes man forget his heavenly
mission and his glorious destiny.

To afford him the means, therefore, of regaining that
position of eminence which he originally maintained
before matter had triumphed over spirit, our Religion
has instituted the two great holy-days—New Year and
Day of Atonement—to act as the means whereby the
end may be attained. For on these days the Israelite
is called upon to examine his past life, to turn his
thoughts from worldly matters, to scrutinize his actions,
to test his moral and religious state, to become conscious of his failings, and to atone for them sincerely
before God. Rosh Hashana, or New Year, called also
Yom Zikaron (Day of Memorial), and Yom Teruah
(Day of the Cornet), is celebrated on the first day of

the seventh month, the commencement of the year being affixed to the autumnal equinox. In the Biblical time, New Year's Day was not kept as such, but was regarded as a festival which was to proclaim the advent of the seventh month, in which the holiest of days (Day of Atonement) and the most joyful of feasts (Feast of Tabernacles) were to be observed, and for this purpose the cornet is ordered to be sounded on that day. At a later period, however, when it was felt necessary to celebrate a feast at the beginning of the year without introducing a new festival for this purpose, it was found the more appropriate and expedient to connect the celebration of this desired New Year's Day with the Day of the Cornet, as this day being the only festival which falls on the first day of the month, and the precursor of the great Day of Atonement, affords the right mood for those serious meditations which the New Year invites. On this day, perhaps more than on any other, we regard God as the King and Judge of the world. We are aroused to a consciousness of His greatness and of our own nothingness, we discover the frailty of life, we acknowledge our proneness to sin, and before the Throne of Grace we humbly confess our failings and transgressions, and implore the Divine forgiveness. Thus is afforded us the opportunity of effecting our peace with Heaven, and of atoning for our sins through the medium of repentance.**

The Day of Atonement (Yom-Hakipurim) is celebrated on the tenth of the seventh month, Tishri, and
is regarded as the holiest of all the days in the year.
Emphatically termed in the Bible the Sabbath of Sabbaths, it imposes upon us the most serious obliga-
tions, for not only must we abstain from all worldly
occupations, but also from all physical enjoyments.
Increased devotional exercises, fervent prayer, a con-
scientious retirement from the outer world, a rigid self-
examination, and an earnest and sincere atonement
are to be the characteristics of that most holy day.
The institution of the Day of Atonement is founded
upon the weakness and the power of man,—upon
the weakness, because man is a human being, and is
liable to the failings of frail mortality;—upon the
power, because man is formed in the image of God,
partakes in a degree of His Divine essence, combines
spirit with matter, and is capable of subduing his material yearnings by the strong will of his spirit.   The
Day of Atonement exemplifies three essential truths
of Judaism : 1. Repentance is necessary to every one,
because there is no one so good as not at some time
to commit sin.   2. God is gracious, all merciful, and
forgiving.   He desires not the death of the wicked,
but rather that they may return to Him and live ;
therefore He pardons the truly repentant sinner and
opens to him the gates of eternal salvation.   3. Man
needs no Mediator to go between him and his God ;

he and he only must and can atone for his sins by repenting and amending his course of conduct."⁹

Therefore are these two great holy-days—New Year and Day of Atonement—regarded by Jews in every part of the world with the greatest reverence, not because they think or believe that God is nearer to them on these days than at any other time in the year, but because they feel that these institutions contain the genuine spirit of religion ; and by removing them for the time being from the thoughts and actions of the world, they are brought nearer to God, by which means they will gain additional strength to conquer the desires of the body, to elevate the qualities of the soul, and thus to approach that state of perfection which is the highest pinnacle of godliness and of supreme felicity.

Thus far have we considered the Holy Seasons as ordained by Moses, and which continue to be regarded as Judaism, because the time has not yet arrived to set them aside.

Besides these, however, we celebrate two half-festivals, instituted in later times in commemoration of some happy events which occurred in the history of Israel. These are the Feast of Purim and the Feast of Channuccah.

The usual avocations of life are permitted on these occasions ; and indeed they partake of no sanctity whatever, being merely historical remembrances, maintained more for the purposes of social and domestic enjoyment than for any intention of especial devotion or religious service.

The Feast of Purim is celebrated on the fourteenth, and in some places of the East on the fifteenth day of the twelfth month, Adar ; except in a leap-year, when it is held on the same days of the thirteenth month, Adar Shenee.

It commemorates the happy deliverance vouchsafed to the Jews in the ancient Persian empire, through the medium of Esther and Mordecai, when the wicked Haman planned the destruction of the Hebrew race throughout the entire dominion of the Persian monarch.

The full history of this event is set forth in detail in the Book of Esther, and is perhaps one of the most pathetic and interesting narratives recorded in the Bible.

The Feast of Channuccah commences with the twenty-fifth day of the ninth month, Kislev, and lasts eight days. It is intended to commemorate the glorious deeds of valor accomplished by the priestly family of the Hasmoneans, and especially by their greatest hero, Judah, surnamed Maccabeus, who after a severe struggle of many years succeeded in effecting the freedom of his people from the Greek tyrant Antiochus Epiphanes, who was then the ruler of Judea. The triumph in this victory consisted in the restoration

of the Jewish religion, which Antiochus had endeavored to exterminate ; for when the immortal Judah
entered Jerusalem, his first care was to repair the
Temple, which had been profaned by the tyrant, to
re-dedicate it, and to illumine it. This event gave rise
to the name of the Feast-Channuccah signifying, Feast
of Dedication. The various incidents connected with
the wars between the Maccabees and Antiochus, together with all the events of the victory, the restoration
and re-dedication, are to be found in the Apocrypha,
in the Books of the Maccabees.

Until recently it was also the custom in Israel to
observe certain fast-days in commemoration of what
was considered as sad events in our past history, and
especially of the fall of Jerusalem and the destruction of the Temple. The fasting on these days, however, was, according to the opinion of the Prophets
and inspired men of Israel, only custom, and no
religious requirement.[70] Of these fasts but one remains, that of the Ninth of Ab, still held as the day
on which the final overthrow of the Jewish nationality
occurred. The others have fallen before the power
of education, increased religious freedom, and the
advance of thought. With the progress of the age,
they have been banished from our religious observances, and are now lost to Israel as they are to the
world. The Ninth of Ab, though by no means observed as a day of fasting and humiliation, is unfor-

tunately maintained, even by those in favor of decided
progress and reform, as a day for serious reflections
and profound solemnity. Whereas it should be considered one of the most joyous days in the Jewish
calendar, for it was indeed a blessing to Israel and to
the world, that the Jewish nationality was overthrown,
the Temple destroyed, and the Jews scattered unto
the four corners of the earth. To Israel it was a
blessing, because thenceforth every Israelite became a
seed, which, sown into different portions of the world,
was hereafter to become a tree, the fruit of which
should even be as the tree of knowledge, giving
instruction to all men. Thenceforth every Israelite
became a missionary of the Most High, to promulgate
His Word of Truth and to diffuse the true Religious
Idea, so as to bring happiness and perfection to the
human race. To the world it was a blessing, because
through the Jews and through Judaism has the world
learnt the knowledge of God, and of those grand
moral laws which have been framed by Him for the
government of His children. To Israel indeed the
world owes all that is good in the respective theories
on religion in which men believe ; and though the
day is yet far distant when mankind will discard the
follies of creed and unite in the pure and holy principles of Religion, truly and surely it is coming,
through the help of Israel, the influence of Judaism,
and the blessing of Almighty God. Surely, then,

when we reflect upon the mighty changes which have been wrought by the hand of time, we cannot feel otherwise than grateful to God for having made us the instruments whereby so much good has been accomplished! Truly the Ninth of Ab, the day when God wisely destroyed our political existence FOREVER; wisely overthrew our Temple and our Temple worship FOREVER; wisely dispersed us among all nations FOREVER,—is becoming more and more recognized as a day of honor and triumph, a day to be commemorated by the purest feelings of joy and gratitude.

And now, having considered the first class of those laws and statutes which have not yet lost their practicability, but which form Judaism according to its temporal phase, we turn to the second class, and proceed to consider The Ceremonies.

The Ceremonies are those outward observances commanded with the intention of rendering us more familiar with the spirit of religion, and accordingly either remind us of events in our past history or of some religious truths. In all cases they are to serve merely as the means to the end, but never are they to usurp the place of the spirit of religion, which alone is capable of rendering our actions acceptable in the sight of God. These Ceremonies may be classified under the following heads : 1st. The Divine Service ; 2d. The rites connected with that service and with the observance of the Festivals ; 3d. The ordinances by which we outwardly attest our high calling, of being a people peculiarly selected and consecrated by God to be His missionaries upon earth.

The Divine Service is founded on the principle that prayer is essential to our happiness, since it affords us the means of communicating with our Heavenly Father, and pouring out to Him the emotions of our souls, thereby rendering us better fitted for the performance of those grand duties of life which are to lead us to perfection and supreme happiness.

This service is either PUBLIC—held in a sanctuary especially devoted and dedicated to that purpose, and in the presence of an assembly of at least ten persons ; or PRIVATE—held alone or in the family circle.

Public worship is of especial importance : first, because it acts as the centre of union of our nation ; and secondly, because the effect thus produced upon the individual cannot be equalled by any private devotion, how solemn or pious soever it may be. The regular assembling together of the individual members of a family, and of many distinct families, in one common house, dedicated to the worship of the same God—the impressions thus produced by this mingling of strangers at the shrine of religion, must tend to foster a love for that religion, and to cement, in a lasting bond of union, the members of that race which is destined to live, dispersed throughout the world, until such time as its glorious mission shall have been accomplished, and all God's children shall belong to one common family and believe in one common religion. Thus public worship acts as the centre of union of our nation. So, also, this scene of an entire congregation united together for the holy purpose of praising God ; the sublime beauty of the prayers ; the solemn and heart-stirring strains of music and song ; and, above all, the spiritual seed sown by the sermon, must take effect upon the individual, and must raise the soul heavenwards in a far greater degree than when in solitude or even in the family circle. Thus, in a spiritual point of view, public worship is likewise to be regarded as possessed of much importance to each and every individual."

Public worship, to be efficacious, should consist of two elements, Devotion and Instruction.

To the former belong : 1. The Confession or Proclamation of God's Unity, called the "Shemang ;" 2. The Prayer proper, called "Tefillah," and containing Praises, Petitions, and Thanks. To the latter belong : 1. Readings from the Law ; 2. Readings from the Prophets ; 3. The Sermon or Religious Discourse.

These elements of the Ritual were instituted by the "Men of the Great Assembly," and were observed even during the existence of the second Temple of Jerusalem. The ritual itself, however, such as has been used until lately by the great mass of Israelites,

was not an emanation from any ecclesiastical author-
ity vested with supreme power, nor was it the produc-
tion of any one distinctive epoch, but was the result
of the gradual formation of many centuries, and the
aggregate of individual contributions.

Hence it is the perfect right of each and every congregation to adopt such ritual as is best adapted to the
spiritual requirements of the members, and is most in
accordance with the demands of the age. The ritual of
the Jews has, as already stated, been the result of the
work of centuries. It is, therefore, not to be wondered
at that it should at length have assumed those gigantic
proportions which characterize the old Minhag of the
so-called Orthodox Jews. Loaded with extracts from the
Mishna and Talmud, replete with needless repetitions
containing sentiments antagonistic to the spirit of the
age, and with petitions the utterance of which in the present period of our history is little better than deliberate
falsehood and blasphemy; it seemed as though the
Jewish idea of prayer was founded on the number of
pages and the bulk of the volume. Whereas Judaism,
even as regarded in its temporal phase, repudiates such
idea, and emphatically maintains that prayer is only
prayer when it proceeds from the heart and is uttered in
that language which is understood by the one who prays.
The very Doctors of the Tradition—those who claim
infallibility for the Talmud—assert that "better is a little
prayer with devotion than a great deal without devo-

tion." [72] Therefore, when the Reform School of Judaism arose and declared that the Ritual of the Jews was a disgrace to Jews, to the age, to the country in which we live, and above all, to the spirit of our Religion, it merely echoed the simple teachings of Judaism ; and it accordingly acted only consistently with those teachings when it discarded the old ritual and prepared others, which should contain the elements prescribed by the "Men of the Great Assembly," while at the same time they should exclude everything unsuitable to our times and condition. Important as have been the changes made within the past quarter of a century, and many as have been the prayer-books written, published, and adopted by individual congregations, there yet exists no form of prayer which is thoroughly in consonance with the spirit of Judaism. Prayer to be efficacious, and to be indeed prayer, must be understood. Now, in a country like ours, where English is the vernacular, where the rising generation of Jews and Gentiles are Americans, English should form no small feature in the public religious services of the Jews. The want of this feature is one of the crying evils which exist in our midst. It is one of the great defects in the prayer-books of the Reform School.

With the exception of but one congregation, [73] the prayers are performed either in Hebrew or in German, or in both. English is altogether ignored. True, most prayer-books contain an English translation, but this surely is not sufficient if that translation is never read in public, or if the Hebrew is not understood. And the Hebrew *is* not understood ; for to their shame be it said, the majority of our brethren are satisfied if their children are able to read the original language without comprehending the meaning of a single word. If, then, the Hebrew tongue is not to be studied—if there is no necessity to impart a knowledge of that language in which the sacred volume is written, if Hebrew is to be entirely expunged from the curriculum of our school studies, then should it be altogether abolished from the sanctuary. There remains, therefore, but one alternative : either public worship must be conducted mainly in English, or it must become a mere pretence to the rising generation, for certainly German is not thoroughly understood by the mass.

To ignore German, however, would be to deprive many of the worshippers of the only means of rendering their prayers truly acceptable ; and to abolish the Hebrew altogether from our services, would be to take away from Israel a very effective means of preserving that union which, from time immemorial, has existed among the members of our scattered people. The time has not yet arrived when Hebrew can be safely dispensed with. Israel must still be a unit ; Israel must still be linked together by the mystic tie of the Hebrew tongue ; for Israelites have still to work

together for the accomplishment of their Heavenly
mission. The time will assuredly arrive when, with
God's blessing, every vestige of error, of idolatry, of
false belief, of bigotry, of superstition, of ignorance,
will be banished from the earth ; when all the petty
differences which various religious systems now build
up, to separate the children of one eternal Father,
will become merged in a lasting bond of union ;
when there will be no more Jews and no more
Christians, no more Mahomedans, no more Pa-
gans ; when the world will no longer resound with
the clamor of opposing doctrines ; but when all
mankind will be regenerated by the universal recognition of God's Divine Rule ; when all mankind will
hail each other as brothers, and rejoice in the glorious
title of Man ; when all the inhabitants of the world
will unite in acknowledging God as the sole and Omnipotent Lord, Ruler, and Savior of His creatures ;
when Peace and Love, Virtue and Knowledge, shall
reign among men ; when there will be but one God
and one Religion, one Kingdom and one Temple,
one Creator and one Human Family. All this will,
undoubtedly, be accomplished in God's own good
time ; for then will be the true Messianic period,
and then will Israel's mission be fulfilled. But, as yet,
the realization of God's gracious promise, foretold by
Israel's prophets through the power of inspiration,
the advent of that glorious event, lies hidden in

the womb of time ; and though we are to-day nearer
to that eventful period than at any past epoch in the
world's history, we are, nevertheless, exceedingly far
from it, and may remain so for ages to come.   Therefore must Israel—the agent through whom this spiritual regeneration of the world is to be effected—still
continue to be united by certain external forces ;
and foremost among these forces is the power of the
Hebrew language.   Enough schisms have taken
place in the camp of Israel, enough differences
exist, enough heart-burnings have been caused.   The
rise, progress, and development of the Reform School
of Judaism have been unwisely permitted to loosen
those ties of love which should bind our people together.   And though we firmly believe in the saying
of our ancient sages, that "every discord, for a holy
purpose, tends in the end to a consolidation,"[74] yet we
cannot but pray to God to put an end to these dis-
cords, and to awaken Israel to a full sense of the position which we are now called upon to take in the
moral race which is agitating the world.   Let not the
Hebrew, then, be abolished from our public religious
services ; but, on the contrary, let it occupy a conspicuous part, so that it may act as the beacon-light
for those poor misguided travellers who are now grop-
ing their way in darkness, and blindly walking in the
paths traced out for them by a mis-styled Orthodoxy,
because they know nothing of the Reform doctrines,

and, in consequence of that ignorance, hate Reform and all its votaries. But, aside from these considerations, once let the Hebrew language be entirely abolished from our religious services, and it will soon cease altogether to be studied. Then will a massive library of literature—which, for beauty of style, profundity of thought, sublimity of sentiment, cannot be equalled by the literature of any nation, profane or sacred—become lost to Israel and to the world.

No! we are not yet ready for the total abolition of Hebrew. Let it remain ; but for the sake of all that is pure and noble, for the sake of virtue and honor, for the sake of religion, for the sake of truth, let it be properly acquired, so that the words of prayer which are put up to Heaven in it, may indeed be prayer, and not a mere hollow outward pretension, a deception of the weakest nature. But while Hebrew is to be thus studied and maintained, it must also be remembered that under existing circumstances, prejudices, and predilections, it would be rather improbable that the mass of Israelites in this country would at once admit and appreciate the necessity for its cultivation and maintenance. Much time would, therefore, have to be consumed before the rising generation would so thoroughly understand the Hebrew language as to be enabled to pray in it. And if even this were so, we have a duty to perform to our Christian breth-

ren in placing before them the doctrines of our faith
and the prayers we offer to our God, in that language
which they best understand.   Now it is altogether impossible for Hebrew ever to become that language,
and it is certainly quite improbable that German will
eventually usurp the place of English.   Be this, however, as it may, it is a fact patent to all, that English
is at the present time the vernacular of these States,
and accordingly English must be employed as the
medium of disseminating our principles, and of giving
utterance to our orisons.   From these considerations
it then becomes evident, that our public Divine Worship, to be truly efficacious, should be performed in
the Hebrew, English, and German languages,—that
is, the prayers should be read in the Hebrew and
English, and the sermon spoken alternately in the
English and German languages.   That the desire
even for German preaching will eventually cease, is,
to us, a settled matter, but until such time arrives, it
would be unwise to deprive a large portion of our
brethren of pulpit instruction.   In holding religious
exercises in two or even more languages, we can see
nothing inconsistent, nothing strange, and certainly
nothing in antagonism to the Jewish Idea.   It is not
necessary to have a uniform Ritual, nor would any
practical good arise therefrom.   At no time in our
history have we had a general Minhag, and it is not
likely we will ever have one, simply because it is not

necessary. Israel can remain a unit without a uniform prayer-book ; but Israel cannot remain a unit if the Hebrew is to be expunged : nor can our public religious services become worthy of the name of Prayers, unless the language of the country, the language which is best understood—English—is used to a ·considerable extent. In this, then, much has to be reformed ere the Reform School of Judaism should be content to repose upon its laurels, and lay down the gauntlet it has taken up in defence of the true Judaic Idea. But still greater evils exist in the manner in which the element of Instruction is fulfilled.

As already stated, Public worship must consist of two elements—Devotion and Instruction ; to the latter of which belong : 1. Readings from the Law. 2. Readings from the Prophets. 3. The sermon or Religious Discourse. Among "so-called" Orthodox Congregations, it is customary to read the Law, by which is meant the Pentateuch or Five Books of Moses, once in every year ; that is, to read a certain portion every Sabbath, beginning with the first chapter of the book of Genesis, and continuing on the following week from the place at which the previous week's portion was terminated, and so on, until the work has been read through to the last verse of Deuteronomy.

According to this rule, an enormous portion of the Bible is recited every Sabbath, the fatigue of which, added to the unbecoming manner in which it is read, and the ridiculous tone of voice or intonation which accompanies it, renders this part of the service intolerably irksome, and consequently devoid of any religious sentiment whatsoever.

Among Reform congregations the reading of the Law is gone through once in every three years, thus materially lessening the weekly Sabbath portions; and in some few congregations, though very few, this is even done once in every seven years. The tri-annual cycle of reading the Law, it may be well to state, was the custom which prevailed in ancient times in the land of Palestine, with the full sanction of the highest ecclesiastical authorities. Important as this reform has been, when compared with the miscalled orthodox system, it yet does not come up to the spirit of the age and the requirements of the Judaic Idea.

Judaism, it must again be asserted, is Religion, and Religion is life, spirit; it is neither letter nor law. The Bible is the word of God only when it is construed from its spiritual signification. There is nothing supernatural about the Bible. It is not a revelation of God's will imparted to any certain man under mysterious circumstances, nor is it a direct communication from God to man. It is a book, and only a book; a book written by mortal hands, a book containing ideas, sentiments, and doctrines emanating from the brain of man. But this by no means diminishes aught from its lustre, since it is the greatest of all works, and bears upon its

face the impress of divinity. For in every passage,
aye, in every word in which the pure spirit of religion
is to be found, there also is the direct work of God,
since He it is who vouchsafed to man those sublime
conceptions of Himself which have been transmitted
to the world through the pages of the Bible. It is in
this way that God communicates His will to man—it
is in this way only that the revelation which is constantly coming to us through the workings of nature
can be fully developed. Wherever then, in the Bible,
the spirit of religion is seen,—wherever the sentiments
which it contains harmonize with the innate sentiment of Religion which God has implanted in the
breast of man, and which becomes gradually more
and more developed according as man comes away
from the dominion of the senses and enters the dominion of the intellect, according as man becomes less
the material being and more the spiritual being,
according as man progresses in reason, in education,
in thought ;—there, indeed, is the Bible the true inspired
word of God, and as such is entitled to our highest
veneration. But the Bible contains, and must ne-
cessarily contain, more than the spirit of Religion,
for being in the first place partly the record of certain
historical events, and partly laws and regulations intended for the government of the Israelitish nation
under especial circumstances ; and in the second place,
being in its details adapted to the requirements of the

people who were contemporaneous with its author or authors, it certainly must contain matter which not only does not partake of the spirit of Religion, but is even devoid of any further interest to us at the present time, than that it affords us the means of studying the past, and becoming acquainted with the history of the growth and development of the Jewish nation and the Judaic Idea. Now, how important or interesting soever such information may be, it surely ought not to be thrust before public notice during Divine worship in the House of God. The very sentiment of devotion must be lessened when the attention is demanded for matters in which the soul can find no enjoyment. Nor is this all ; for the careful reader of the Bible must know that there are many chapters which are positively unfit to be read aloud in a public assemblage, and which certainly would not be tolerated in decent society if read aloud in English. Why, then, ought they to be permitted in the Hebrew language ? Is this not in itself positive proof that the Hebrew is not understood, and that consequently this portion of the service is a mockery and deception ?

It is, indeed, sad to find how people, although decidedly in favor of progress and reform, can be so wedded to the past as to be content to permit such anomalies to be presented to the world under the garb of Judaism.

The Reform School has yet to accomplish the task

of amending the Scriptural portions recited in public
during the hours of divine service ; and this can easily
be done, either by expunging from the biblical portions such as are unfit for our times and condition, or
by ceding to the Clergymen of the respective houses
of worship the right of determining what chapters
shall be recited aloud in the sanctuary.   In like manner, also, should the Readings from the Prophets be
regulated.   The Prophets were, indeed, the chosen
depositaries, the agents of the true religious Idea ; and
their beautiful words of inspiration portray their deep
love for their God, their religion, and their country,
and exhibit in bright colors the magnificent conceptions they formed of Israel's calling and Israel's
glorious destiny.   Truly it may be said, that Israel's
greatest Reformers were the Prophets.   Yet even their
writings should not be indiscriminately read aloud in
the Sanctuary.   Care should be taken in the selection
of the passages, so that nothing might be introduced
into the service which is not fully adapted to our time,
condition, and requirements.

As essential as the Readings from the Law and the
Prophets, is the Sermon, or Religious Discourse.
No house of worship should be without its regular
Preacher.   The institution of the Pulpit is one of the
oldest in Judaism.   It was original in our faith, and
has from us been borrowed by the followers of all
religious systems.   It therefore becomes our bounden

duty to foster this institution, to labor for it, and to maintain it, as one of the greatest auxiliaries to the Jewish Idea. Until within comparatively late years, however, the Jews of this country have not been fully sensible of the great advantages to be derived from the Pulpit; and even at the present day, the Jewish Pulpit of the United States is in a very unsatisfactory condition; for in many of our Synagogues there exists no pulpit at all, and, with but few exceptions, those which maintain pulpits do so only in the German language. Now, all that has been said about the necessity of conducting the ritual mainly in English will apply just as forcibly to the Pulpit. Vernacular preaching in this country is indispensable, if the Reform School of Judaism desires to continue the holy work of disseminating the true Judaic Idea, and of bringing Jews and Gentiles to one common faith. There are certainly a few preachers who speak to the people in the English language; but of these few, only four are enabled to claim the English as their mother tongue. Yet there are over two hundred congregations in the United States.

This great want will soon have to be supplied; for a marked change is coming over our people, and the desire for English discourses is being daily manifested. Already some of the leading Congregations have taken measures towards obtaining the services of divines capable of preaching in the vernacular,

and have, praiseworthily, determined to support an
English as well as a German Pulpit, so that the requirements of all classes will be properly fulfilled.
So soon as the great majority of Congregations shall
have progressed so far as to have arrived at this stage ;
so soon as a proper ritual shall have been adopted,
which will effectually answer our time and condition,
so soon will the Public Worship of the Jews be in accordance with the spirit of Judaism and the object for
which Public Worship is held.

Upon the subject of Private Worship, but few words
are necessary.   In this, as in our public services, the
prayers we offer up to the Throne of Grace must
not be mere lip-service, performed so as to keep
within the letter of the law, but must spring from the
heart, and be the genuine offspring of a pious mind.
Accordingly, it would not be desirable to fix any one
particular form of prayer to be used at our private de-
votions, in preference to any other form.   Our own
prayers, which flow spontaneously from the soul, and
which are sent upward by the breath of sincerity, how
poor soever the language may be, are the more acceptable, in the sight of Him who readeth the heart,
than all the eloquent and learned effusions we may
utter, if unaccompanied with that true devotional feeling, which can alone render the words which escape
our lips words of prayer.   Yet while this freedom is
allowed to the individual, and it is optional with him

to pray when and in what manner his own feelings
prompt, it would be well for us all to accustom ourselves to regular devotional exercises, morning and
evening, and at meal-time. Indeed, the Bible gives
some intimation of this, in many passages.[76]

The reading of the Bible and other religious books,
also comes under the head of private worship, and
forms one of the most efficacious means of preserving
man's communion with God, and guarding him
against sinking into complete worldliness. Thus
through Divine Worship, be it Public or Private, man
is constantly reminded of his divine origin, of his
immortal soul, and of his heavenly destiny ; and by
thus being trained to direct his thoughts above the
material desires and cravings of life, he is led on the
road to perfection and to supreme happiness.

The second division of The Ceremonies, as already
stated, comprises the rites connected with the Divine
service, and with the observance of the Festivals.

These rites—which are nothing more than those
outward manifestations which all ceremonial religion
adopts, in order to impress the minds of the people,
and especially those of the uneducated classes, more
strongly with the nature of the service—have gradually diminished before the efforts of the Reform
School, and will, doubtless, vanish altogether before
another generation shall have passed from earth.

Those which still remain among us to show that

we have not yet arrived at a proper appreciation of the true inherent beauties of Judaism, are : first, the sounding of the Cornet on New Year's Day ; second, the exhibition of the Festive wreath during the Feast of Tabernacles ; and third, the kindling of extra lights on the Festival of Channuccah. Besides these rites, which are openly performed in the House of Worship, we have the following : 1. Abstinence from leavened bread on the Feast of Passover. 2. The eating of unleavened bread on the first night of this Feast. 3. The fast on the Day of Atonement. Among the most progressive of our co-religionists, however, the first has already commenced to fall into desuetude.

The third division of The Ceremonies is, the ordinances by which we outwardly attest our high calling of being a people peculiarly selected and consecrated by God to be His missionaries upon earth.

These Ordinances, which were also given by Moses for certain wise purposes, and were to remain operative so long as the times and condition of the Israelites demanded them, have, like the Rites, become by degrees abrogated, until the only one which now remains is The Circumcision.

This ordinance does not properly come under the category of ordinances given by Moses, since it dates back to the days of Abraham, who, according to the Bible, first conceived the idea of thus implanting in the flesh the seal of the covenant—in other words, of thus pre-eminently distinguishing Israel as a peculiar people, selected and appointed for some especial purpose." It has, therefore, at all times been regarded with great veneration, and will, most probably, endure longer than any other of the Ceremonial Laws.   That it must fall eventually, however, is as certain as that the heavens and the earth exist.   And when the time shall have arrived for the nations of the earth—the children of One Eternal God—to be brought nearer to each other, and thus to fulfil the gracious promise of the Almighty—that through Israel all the families of the world shall be blessed—then truly will this ceremony have been abrogated and placed among the relics of a past age.

To hasten this glorious event should now be the aim and hope of Israel.   We have seen that Judaism, regarded in its Eternal phase, is, indeed, pure religion, and is destined to become the faith in which all the world will eventually believe.   We have seen also that Judaism in its temporal phase, even as maintained by the Reform School, is yet capable of much improvement ere it is in full accordance with the spirit of the age and the true spirit of Religion.   It behooves us then to unite heart and soul in purging our faith from the impurities of the past—impurities which tarnish its lustre and serve only as impediments to the fulfilment of our heavenly mission.   Yes, Israelites, ours is a glorious mission, a God-like destiny, a brilliant future ! Much have we already done towards the elevation of mankind, but much more has yet to be accomplished. As the missionaries of the Most High, we have been constant in our calling, and willingly or unwillingly, we have been compelled to work out His grand idea of universal fraternity. We have taught the world sublime truths under all circumstances and conditions : when in the enjoyment of an independent political nationality, and when as captives on the soil of our conquerors ; when as aliens in strange lands, down trodden and oppressed by our fellow-creatures, and when as citizens in those states and countries over which the flag of liberty floats.

Ever true to the leading fundamental idea of Judaism—the Unity of God—we have in all ages and climes adopted such outward aids to Religion as were most conducive to the preservation of the inward spirit. Let us then not flinch from our mission, now that God has blessed our cause and opened to us the way of reaching the hearts of the nations by whom we are surrounded. At no past epoch in the world's history have the chances been as favorable for the dissemination of the Judaic Idea, as they are at the present time. Let us avail ourselves then of the opportunity ; let us remove the bar which exists between man and man ; let us, by our own acts, give the world, upon the subject of our Religion, that best of lessons—the lesson of example, and thus draw nearer and nearer to us our non-Jewish brethren, until at last all those petty prejudices which ignorance, bigotry, and superstition have established to separate the children of one common Father, become merged in an eternal bond of union.

Then will the words of the Prophet be realized, "On that day will the Eternal be acknowledged One and His name be One."[77]

May the Almighty Parent of all, in His infinite mercy and love for His creatures, hasten that eventful day, and so promote the happiness of Israel, the happiness of mankind, and the glory and honor of His great, good, and hallowed name, which we most fervently praise and bless now and evermore.

NOTES AND REFERENCES.

[1] "I the Lord have called thee in righteousness, and will lay hold on thy hand and will keep thee and appoint thee *for a covenant of the people*, for a light of the nations." (Isaiah xlii. 6.)

[2] Maimonides.

[3] Sir William Hamilton.

[4] Pensées, p. 1, art. iv., § 6.

[5] "The fool saith in his heart there is no God." (Ps. xiv. 1.)

[6] The greatest thinkers of ancient and modern times entertain the opinion that man's happiness does not consist so much in the actual fulfilment of his desires as in the excitement of the pursuit; in other words, that man's happiness can only be produced by continual progression. Thus Aristotle says, "The intellect is perfected, not by knowledge, but by activity." Plato defines man "the hunter of truth." "If," says Malebranche, "I held truth captive in my hand, I should open my hand and let it fly, in order that I might again pursue and capture it." So also Lessing remarks, "Did the Almighty, holding in his right hand Truth, and in his left Search after Truth, deign to tender me the one I might prefer, in all humility, but without hesitation, I should request Search after Truth." "Truth," says Von Müller, "is the property of God, the pursuit of truth is what belongs to man;" and in like manner Jean Paul Richter says, "It is not the goal, but the course which makes us happy." Compare Sir William Hamilton's Lectures on Logic, Lect. 1, p. 8.

[7] "And the Lord said unto Abraham: Get thee out

of thy country. . . . . *and in thee all the generations of the earth shall be blessed.*" (Genesis xii. 1–3.)

Vide Deut. ch. 4, especially v. 6, as follows: "Keep therefore and do them ; for this is your wisdom and your understanding before the eyes of the nations, that shall hear all these statutes, and will say, Nothing but a wise and understanding people is this great nation."

"And ye shall be unto me a kingdom of priests, and a holy nation." (Exodus xix. 6.)

Isaiah xlii. 6, as in note 1.

[8] Even in the Rabbinical works, which often contain very bigoted and exclusive ideas upon several subjects, the great truth is told that man is responsible to God alone for his religious belief. "The pious of all creeds," say the fathers, "have a share in the future world." The doctrine that belief in one particular creed is essential to salvation is nowhere to be found in Judaism. If, therefore, so much freedom of thought is ceded to our neighbors, and the grand, leading idea of Judaism is the universal recognition of God and of the Moral Law, it surely follows that in the mission of our race there can be no exclusiveness, but that the divine blessings of our Religion are destined to become the common inheritance of mankind.

[9] "And God said unto Moses : Thou canst not see my face, for no man can see me and live." (Exodus xxxiii. 20.)

[10] "Holy, holy, holy is the Lord of hosts, the whole earth is full of his glory." (Isaiah vi. 3.)

"Every word of God is pure." (Proverbs xxx. 5.)

"As for God, His way is perfect." (2 Sam. xxii. 31.)

[11] "The heavens and the heaven of heavens cannot contain Thee." (1 Kings viii. 27.)

"And take ye good heed unto yourselves, for ye saw no form on the day that God spoke unto you on Horeb from out of the fire." (Deut. iv. 15.)

[12] "Before the mountains were brought forth, and ere thou hadst formed the earth and the world, even from everlasting to everlasting thou art God." (Psalm xc. 2.)

"I the Eternal, I change not." (Malachi iii. 6.)

[13] "Hear, O Israel, the Lord our God is One Eternal God." (Deut. iv. 39.)

" Know this day, and reflect in thy heart, that the Lord
is God in the heaven above and on the earth beneath,
there is none else." (Deut. iv. 29.)

" To whom will ye liken and assimilate me, and compare me, that we may be like?" (Isaiah xlvi. 5.)

[14] " He spoke, and it was done; He commanded, and
it stood." (Psalm xxxiii. 9.)

" He doth great things, which cannot be searched out,
and wonders without number." (Job ix. 10.)

[15] " Before a word was on my tongue, thou, O Lord,
didst know all." (Psalm cxxxix. 4.)

" The eyes of God survey the whole world." (Zechariah
iv. 10.)

" The Lord hath with wisdom formed the earth, and
with understanding established the heavens." (Prov. iii.
10.)

[16] " Can any one hide himself, and I not see him, saith
the Lord, do I not fill the heavens and the earth?" (Jer.
xxiii. 24.) Compare Psalm cxxxix. 7–10.

[17] " Good is the Lord towards all, and his mercy is over
all his creatures." (Psalm cxlv. 9.)

" The Rock—His work is perfect, for all His ways
are just." (Deut. xxxii. 5.)

" Far it is from God, that he should act wrongfully,
and from the Almighty that he should do injustice."
(Job xxxiv. 10.)

[18] " For as heaven is exalted above the earth, so are
my ways higher than your ways, and my thoughts than
your thoughts." (Isaiah lv. 9.)

" The Lord hath with wisdom formed the earth, and
with understanding established the heavens." (Proverbs
iii. 10.)

[19] " The Lord, the Lord is a merciful and gracious
God, long-suffering and abundant in goodness and truth ;
he forgiveth iniquity, transgression, and sin." (Exodus
xxxiv. 6–7.)

[20] " Thou openest thy hand and satisfiest the desire of
every living creature." (Psalm cxlv. 16.)

[21] " And God said unto Moses: I AM WHO I AM."
(Exodus iii. 14.)

[22] " In the beginning God created the heaven and the

earth." (Gen. i. I.) Compare Psalm xc. 2; Isaiah xlvi. 9–10.

. . . "But thou art ever the same, and thy years will have no end." (Psalm cii. 25–28.)

[23] "Thus hath said the Lord, the King of Israel, and his Redeemer, the Lord of Hosts; I am the first and I am the last; and beside me there is no God." (Isaiah xlv. 6; also Isaiah xli. 4.)

[24] Compare Psalm civ.

[25] "Lift up your eyes and look. Who hath created these things?" (Isaiah xl. 26.) Compare Job xii. 7–10.

[26] "The Lord is King for ever and ever." (Psalm x. 16.)

"Even Thou art Lord alone." (Neh. ix. 6; Isaiah xxxvii. 20.)

"He turneth the changes by his counsels," &c. (Job xxxvii. 12.)

"For in his hand is the soul of all living and the spirit of all flesh." (Job xii. 10.)

"O Eternal, thou preservest man and beast." (Psalm xxxvi. 6.)

[27] "For thus saith the Lord: the Creator of heaven is God," &c. (Isaiah xlv. 18.)

[28] "I am Lord, besides me there is no Saviour." (Isaiah xlii. 11.)

"There is no Saviour beside me." (Hos. xiii. 4.)

[29] "In the beginning God created the heaven and the earth." (Gen. i. 1.)

[30] "God hath created all things to respond to His purposes." (Prov. xvi. 4.)

[31] "The Lord hath with wisdom formed the earth." (Prov. iii. 10.)

[32] "And God surveyed all that He had made, and behold it was very good." (Gen. i. 31.)

[33] "Your thoughts are not my thoughts, neither are your ways my ways." (Isaiah iv. 8.)

[34] "The world is built up in mercy." (Psalm lxxxix. 2.)

[35] "And God created man from the dust of the earth and breathed into him a living soul." (Genesis ii. 7.)

"In the likeness of God hath He created man." (Gen. i. 27.)

" And dust returneth into dust, as it was, but the spirit returneth unto God who gave it." (Ecclesiastes xii. 7.)

[36] " Life and death, blessing and cursing, I have set before thee ; choose life !" (Deut. xxx. 19.)

" Walk before me and be thou perfect." (Gen. xvii. 1.) Compare Proverbs ii. 10, 11.

[37] " For the imagination of man is evil from his youth." (Gen. viii. 21.)

[38] " Sin lieth at the door, and after thee is its desire, but thou canst rule over it." (Genesis iv. 7.)

[39] " And the wicked are like the troubled sea, that cannot rest, and of which the waters cast up mire and dirt. There is no peace, saith the Lord, to the wicked." (Isaiah lvii. 20, 21.)

[40] Compare Ezekiel xxxiii. 10–20 and Isaiah lv. 6, 7.

[41] " And thou shalt love the Lord thy God with all thy heart, and with all thy soul, and with all thy might." (Deut. vi. 5.)

[42] " O Lord our God, how excellent is Thy name in all the earth." (Psalm viii. 1.)

[43] " Fear God and keep his commandments, for this is the whole duty of man." (Ecclesiastes xii. 13.)

[44] " How good and how beautiful it is for brethren to dwell together in unity ; for there the Lord will command the blessing and life to dwell evermore." (Psalm cxxxiii. 1–3.)

[45] . . . . " What is man that thou art mindful of him . . . ?" (Psalm viii. 1–4.)

" Good is the Eternal to all, and His mercy is over all His works." (Psalm cxlv. 9.)

" Whom God loveth he chastiseth." (Proverbs iii. 12.)

" We should thank God for the good as well as for the evil." (Mishna, Berachoth, ix. 5.)

" Trust in the Lord with all thy heart, and rely not on thy intellect." (Prov. iii. 5.)

" Give thanks unto the Lord, for he is good." (Psalm cxviii. 1.)

[46] Compare Isaiah lviii. 6, 7 ; Deut. xv. 7, 8.

[47] " Thou shalt not avenge nor bear a grudge." (Levit. xix. 18.)

[48] "If a stranger sojourn with you in your land, you shall not afflict him. . . . thou shalt love him as thyself." (Levit. xix. 43.)

[49] "Thou shalt love thy *neighbor* as thyself." (Levit. xix. 18.)

"Have we not all one Father? Hath not one God created us?" (Malachi xii. 10.)

Besides the general duties to our fellow-creatures, our Religion prescribes particular duties to be observed in all the social relations of life. Of these the following are the principal divisions: Husbands and wives; parents and children; teachers and pupils; masters and servants; state and citizen. The biblical authorities upon these duties are too numerous for insertion, but can be easily found in the books of Exodus and Leviticus.

[50] "When wisdom entereth into thine heart, and knowledge is pleasant to thy soul, discretion shall preserve thee, and understanding shall keep thee." (Prov. ii. 10, 11.)

[51] "Teach my words to your children," &c. (Deut. xi. 19.)

"The fear of the Lord is the beginning of wisdom." (Prov. i. 7.)

[52] "The Eternal God took man and placed him in the garden of Eden to cultivate it." (Gen. ii. 15.)

"The soul of the diligent shall be made fat." (Prov. xiii. 4.)

"And ye shall not follow the inclinations of your hearts and of your eyes, after which ye are wont to go astray." (Numbers xv. 39.)

"Ye shall be holy, for I, the Lord your God, am holy." (Levit. xix. 2.)

"Keep my commandments, that thou mayest live." (Proverbs vii. 2.)

"Be watchful of thy heart above everything." (Prov. iv. 23.)

[53] Genesis iii. 10.

[54] Genesis iv. 4.

[55] Genesis iv. 7.

[56] Compare Genesis xxii.

[57] Genesis xxvi. 25; xxxiii. 20; xl. 8; xli. 16; xlvi. 1.

[58] The Egyptians, Grecians, and Romans had their Religions, and how simple or imperfect soever their Mythology may have been, it was yet the result of that religious sentiment innate in the human breast.

[59] When Judaism arose, nearly all the nations by which the Israelites were surrounded offered human sacrifices to their gods, and this fact is fully proved from the biblical commands respecting Moloch, and the charge, repeated so often, "Not to go after the gods of the nations."

[60] No greater proof of this need be given than the fact of the Israelites having compelled Aaron to make the golden calf, before which they exclaimed, "These are thy gods, O Israel, that have brought thee up out of the land of Egypt." (Exodus xxxii.)

[61] Jeremiah vii. 22.

[62] Mishna, Taanith, iv. 2.

[63] "Verily my Sabbaths ye shall keep, for it is a sign between me and you," &c. (Exodus xxxi. 13–18.)

Compare Gen. ii. 1–3.

"Remember the Sabbath day to keep it holy," &c. (Exodus xx. 8–11.)

"If thou restrain thy foot for the sake of the Sabbath, not doing thy business on my holy day; and if thou call the Sabbath a delight, the holy day of the Lord honorable, and honor it by not doing thy usual pursuits, by not following thy own words and speaking vain words." (Isaiah lviii. 13.)

[64] Compare Exodus xii., especially the following passages: "Seven days shall ye eat only unleavened bread." (15.)

"And on the first day there shall be unto you a holy convocation, and on the seventh day there shall be unto you a holy convocation." (16.)

"In the first month on the fourteenth day of the month at even ye shall eat only unleavened bread, until the twenty-first day of the month at even." (18.)

"It was a night of Watch unto the Lord from bringing them out of the land of Egypt; this night therefore is holy to the Lord, a memorial unto all the children of Israel, for their generations." (42.)

[65] Compare Leviticus xxiii. 15–22.

"Seven weeks shalt thou number; from the time thou beginnest to put the sickle to the corn, shalt thou begin to number seven weeks." (Deut. xvi. 9–12.)

Mishna, Rosh Hashana, i. 2.

[66] Right Rev. Arthur P. Stanley, D. D. Lectures on the History of the Jewish Church. Lect. vii. p. 198.

[67] Leviticus xxiii. 33, to the end of the chapter.

[68] "In the seventh month, on the first day of the month, shall ye have a rest, a day of memorial of sounding the cornet, a holy convocation." (Levit. xxiii. 24.) Vide Numbers xxix. 1.

[69] "In the seventh month, on the tenth of the month, ye shall afflict yourselves, and do no manner of work, both the native and the stranger who dwelleth amongst you; for on that day he atoneth for you to purify you—from all your sins ye shall purify yourselves before God. It shall be a Sabbath of Sabbaths unto you." (Levit. xvi. 29–31.) Vide Levit. xxiii. 32.

[70] "Speak ye unto all the people of the land and to the priests, saying, When ye fasted and mourned in the fifth and seventh month even those seventy years, did ye at all fast for my sake? These are the things that ye shall do: speak ye the truth every man to his neighbor, execute the judgment of truth and peace in your gates. Thus hath said the Lord of Hosts: The fast of the fourth, and the fast of the fifth, and the fast of the seventh, and the fast of the tenth months shall become to the house of Judah gladness and joy and merry festivals, only love ye the truth and peace." (Zechariah vii. 5; viii. 16, 19.)

[71] "My Sabbaths shall ye keep, and my *Sanctuary* shall ye reverence. I am the Lord." (Levit. xix. 30.)

"I rejoiced when they said unto me, Let us go to the house of the Lord." (Psalm cxxii. 1.)

[72] Shulchan·Arooch. Oro Chayim, i. 4.

[73] Temple Emanu-El.

[74] Mishna, Aboth, v. 17.

[75] "O Lord, in the morning do Thou hear my voice." (Psalms v. 4; lix. 16; lv. 17, 18; Deut. vi. 11, 12.)

[76] Genesis xvii. 9–27.

[77] Zechariah xiv. 9.